NAVIGATING DIGITAL TRANSFORMATION IN THE MODERN ERA

ELMER SHERMAN

Copyright © 2024 ELMER SHERMAN

All rights reserved. No part of this book may be reproduced, distributed, or transmitted in any form or by any means, including photocopying, recording, or other electronic or mechanical methods, without the prior written permission of the publisher, except in the case of brief quotations embodied in critical reviews and certain other noncommercial uses permitted by copyright law.

TABLE OF CONTENTS

INTRODUCTION
    Recognizing Digital Transformation in Various Sectors
    Digital Banking's Contribution to the Transformation of Financial Services
    Digital Disruption in the Petroleum Sector
    Harnessing Big Data for Competitive Advantage

Part I: DETERMINING THE TRANSFORMATION STAGE
    Evaluating Organizational Culture
    Developing a Vision for Banking's Digital Revolution
    Modernizing Petroleum Sector Procedures for the Digital Age

Part II: TECHNOLOGY FOUNDATIONS
    Utilizing Digital Platforms for Banking Activities
    IoT and Automation in the Petroleum Industry
    Big Data Analytics

Part III: IMPROVING THE USER INTERFACE
    Design Thinking for Products and Services in Digital Banking
    Enhancing User Interface for Petroleum Operations
    Personalization Strategies for Customer Engagement

Part IV: FOSTERING AN DIGITAL CULTURE
    Effective Leadership Techniques to Promote Digital Adoption
    Encouraging Innovation in Petroleum and Banking Sectors
    Retraining Employees in Digital Competence

Part V: IMPLEMENTATION AND EXECUTION
    Agile Project Management Techniques for Digital Banking
    Overcoming Resistance to Change in the Petroleum Industry
    Overseeing Digital Transformation Initiatives at Large

Part VI: BEYOND DIGITAL TRANSFORMATION
    Ethical Aspects in Banking and Petroleum Operations
    Prospects for the Future of Petroleum Technologies and Digital Banking
    Case Studies: Insights from Effective Digital Revolutions

CONCLUSION

INTRODUCTION

How does digital transformation work?

Through the integration of digital technology, corporate processes, models, and operations are fundamentally reimagined and restructured through digital transformation. It comprises utilizing state-of-the-art digital technologies and platforms to improve customer experiences, efficiency, and innovation in every aspect of an organization. Fundamentally, digital transformation is a calculated reaction to the speed at which technology is developing as well as the evolving expectations of stakeholders and customers in the current digital era.

Fundamentally, digital transformation goes beyond simple digitization or process automation. While digitization entails transforming analog data into digital representations, digital transformation takes a step farther and radically changes how companies function and provide value to their clients. In order to drive innovation, agility, and competitiveness, it means embracing digital technology as essential parts of the organization's DNA rather than as supplements or add-ons.

An organization's internal procedures and culture as well as its outward contacts with partners, suppliers, and customers are all impacted by digital transformation. It entails utilizing cutting-edge technologies like blockchain, Internet of Things (IoT), artificial intelligence, data analytics, and cloud computing to improve decision-making, expedite processes, and create new avenues for expansion and distinction.

Meeting the changing requirements and expectations of customers in an increasingly digital world is one of the main forces behind the digital transformation. Consumers of today expect smooth, customized, and convenient experiences through all touchpoints and channels. By using data-driven insights to comprehend customer behavior, preferences, and pain points and by creating innovative products, services, and experiences that are catered to their needs, digital transformation helps firms meet and exceed these expectations.

Furthermore, companies can become more agile and responsive to shifting market conditions and competitive demands thanks to digital transformation. Organizations can adopt digital technologies to expedite decision-making, automate tedious procedures, and streamline workflows. This allows them to quickly adjust to changing market conditions, client input, and emerging opportunities.

Moreover, via innovation and diversification, digital transformation helps businesses to open up new income streams and sources of value. Organizations can access new markets, generate new revenue streams, and produce cutting-edge goods and services that satisfy changing consumer demands and market demands by utilizing digital platforms and ecosystems.

Digital change is not without its difficulties, though. It calls for an all-encompassing, integrated strategy that takes into account people, technology, processes, and culture. To properly begin their digital transformation journey, organizations must overcome old systems and procedures, handle regulatory difficulties, and deal with cultural opposition to change.

In the current digital era, digital transformation denotes a significant change in the way firms create, function, and provide value. In an increasingly competitive and dynamic business market, firms can unlock new potential for development and distinction by embracing digital technology, which can improve efficiency, agility, and customer experiences. But to really achieve the benefits of digital transformation, one needs a clear strategic direction, capable leadership, and a dedication to ongoing innovation and adaptability.

Digital transformation has become a key factor in today's quickly changing corporate environment, propelling innovation and changing sectors worldwide. Organizations are negotiating the digital terrain in a world that is becoming more and more digital, from energy to banking, to stay relevant and competitive. This in-depth investigation delves into the complex domain of digital transformation, scrutinizing its influence on a range of industries, including banking and petroleum. We also look at how important big data is to maintaining a competitive edge in the face of digital upheaval.

Recognizing Digital Transformation in Various Sectors

It is true that digital transformation cuts across all industries, changing customer experiences and corporate assumptions. Digital transformation has sparked a revolution in the way financial institutions interact with their clients and carry out their business in the financial services industry, especially in banking.

Online banking systems have made financial services more accessible to a wider range of people by removing geographical and temporal limitations. Through mobile banking apps, customers can now easily monitor their accounts, transfer money, and pay bills either at home or on the move. In addition to improving client convenience, this move to digital channels has allowed banks to save operating expenses related to staffing and maintaining physical locations.

Furthermore, the shift to a cashless society has been expedited by the emergence of digital wallets and mobile payment systems. Customers may divide bills, send money to friends and family, and make purchases with just a few clicks on their iPhones. In addition to revolutionizing consumer behavior, this ease of use has allowed banks to generate new income streams through merchant partnerships and transaction fees.

Another game-changing development in the financial services sector are robo-advisors, which provide regular clients with automated portfolio management and investment guidance. At a fraction of the cost of traditional financial counselors, robo-advisors can deliver individualized investment recommendations by utilizing machine learning and algorithmic techniques to assess investors' risk profiles and investment objectives. The democratization of wealth management has reduced fees and improved accessibility to investment options, giving people the power to take charge of their financial futures.

Moreover, banks can now better understand client behavior and preferences by utilizing data analytics thanks to the digital transformation. Banks are able to enhance client retention, customize marketing efforts, and personalize their services by examining transactional data, social media interactions, and demographic data. In addition to improving client satisfaction, this data-driven approach to banking helps banks to detect fraudulent activity, identify and reduce risks, and improve regulatory compliance.

All things considered, digital transformation has completely changed the banking sector, allowing banks to provide their clients with more individualized, convenient, and secure services while increasing operational effectiveness and cutting costs. To stay ahead of the curve in an increasingly digital environment, banks must continue to be flexible and inventive as technology and client expectations change.

Digital Banking's Contribution to the Transformation of Financial Services

Within the larger context of digital transformation, digital banking is driving significant changes in the financial services industry that fundamentally affect the way people manage their finances. The way clients access and manage their financial resources has been revolutionized by the seamless integration of technology into traditional banking operations, which is at the heart of this shift.

The emergence of smartphones and widespread internet connectivity has brought about an unparalleled level of convenience and accessibility in the banking industry. Customers can perform a wide range of financial operations with unmatched convenience and efficiency using digital banking platforms, which go beyond geographical limitations and conventional banking hours. Customers may now manage their finances on their own terms, whenever and wherever they choose, by using mobile banking apps to deposit checks, pay bills, and transfer money between accounts.

Moreover, the financial industry benefits greatly from the innovation and disruption that digital banking brings. Fintech companies are revolutionizing the financial services industry by questioning established banking paradigms and reshaping it with their innovative technologies and agile business models. Peer-to-peer lending platforms, digital wallets, and blockchain-based payment systems are just a few examples of the disruptive technologies that are changing consumer expectations and forcing established banks to change or risk going out of business.

In this new era of digital banking, cooperation between traditional banks and fintech startups has become strategically vital. In order to be competitive in a market that is getting more and more crowded, banks understand that they must embrace innovation and make use of outside knowledge. Banks may take use of fintech firms' specialized knowledge and technological solutions by collaborating with them, quickening the rate of innovation and promoting digital transformation in the sector.

But the emergence of digital banking also presents traditional financial organizations with a number of new issues and concerns. The most important of these is the need to strengthen cybersecurity defenses in order to protect sensitive financial data and fend off changing cyberattacks. To maintain the security and integrity of their digital banking systems, banks need to invest in strong cybersecurity infrastructure and standards given the growth of digital channels and the complexity of digital transactions.

For banks working in the digital space, managing regulatory obligations and compliance standards is also a major concern. The swift advancement of technology frequently surpasses the speed of regulatory structures, causing banks to struggle with matters of adherence to regulations and unpredictability. Banks must take a proactive approach to compliance in order to reduce these risks. They must install strong governance frameworks and keep a close eye on regulatory developments in order to guarantee that legal and regulatory obligations are followed.

Notwithstanding these difficulties, digital banking has indisputable advantages that present the financial services sector with never-before-seen chances for expansion, productivity, and client interaction. Banks can take the lead in innovation and create value for stakeholders and consumers in the increasingly digital world by embracing digital transformation and utilizing technology.

Digital Disruption in the Petroleum Sector

Amidst the unrelenting march of digital disruption, the petroleum industry, a pillar of global energy production and economic growth, finds itself at a crossroads. Previously distinguished by its dependence on tangible infrastructure and manual procedures, the sector is currently experiencing a profound upheaval driven by swift progress in digital technology.

Automation, the Internet of Things (IoT), and data analytics are transforming every aspect of the petroleum value chain, and they are at the center of this transition. Digital technologies are driving efficiency benefits, enhancing decision-making processes, and opening up new potential for value creation in a variety of industries, from exploration and production to refining and distribution.

The need to optimize operations and save costs in a market that is becoming more and more competitive is one of the biggest problems facing the petroleum industry. Numerous solutions are available to tackle this difficulty with digital technology, ranging from real-time monitoring and production process optimization to predictive maintenance employing

Internet of Things sensors. Oil and gas firms can improve their competitiveness and profitability by identifying operational inefficiencies, minimizing downtime, and maximizing asset performance through the utilization of data-driven insights.

Additionally, the petroleum business has a rare chance to embrace sustainability and lessen its environmental impact thanks to the digital transformation. There is increasing pressure on oil and gas businesses to embrace more sustainable and cleaner methods due to growing worries about climate change and environmental deterioration. Through the utilization of renewable energy sources, integration of energy-efficient technologies, and streamlining production procedures, businesses can simultaneously enhance their environmental footprint and cut expenses.

The path towards digital transformation is not without difficulties, though. The adoption of digital technologies is hindered significantly by legacy infrastructure, which is comprised of equipment and systems that are decades old. It takes significant resources and experience to retrofit existing infrastructure with digital sensors and connection technologies, and a phased implementation strategy is frequently required.

Furthermore, a plethora of municipal, federal, and international regulations oversee the petroleum industry's operations within a complicated regulatory environment. For oil and gas firms looking to embrace digital transformation, navigating these regulations, making sure they are followed, and getting the required permits and clearances can be difficult tasks.

Another major obstacle to digital transformation in the petroleum business is cultural resistance to change. Since many workers in the sector are used to operating in old methods, they could be reluctant to adopt new tools and procedures. Strong leadership, clear communication, and extensive training programs that guarantee staff members have the abilities and knowledge required to thrive in the digital age are all necessary to overcome this opposition.

Furthermore, in a society that is becoming more digitally connected and integrated, cybersecurity risks are significant. As digital infrastructure and data-driven technologies proliferate, new vulnerabilities are created that bad actors might take advantage of. Strong cybersecurity measures are essential for oil and gas firms to protect their digital assets and prevent breaches, which might have serious repercussions for reputation, operational integrity, and safety.

In summary, the petroleum business has both opportunities and problems as a result of digital disruption. Businesses can lower their environmental impact, increase operational efficiency, and improve decision-making processes by adopting digital transformation. But in order to succeed in the digital age, it's imperative to overcome outdated infrastructure, manage regulatory complications, deal with cultural resistance, and reduce cybersecurity risks.

Harnessing Big Data for Competitive Advantage

Data has become a strategic asset for businesses looking to acquire a competitive edge and spur innovation in the age of digital transformation. Big data, which is defined by its volume, velocity, and diversity, presents a great deal of opportunity for businesses in a range of sectors to gain new insights, improve decision-making, and spur expansion.

Big data analytics helps banks to better understand consumer behavior, preferences, and trends in the financial services industry. Through the examination of copious amounts of transactional data, social media interactions, and demographic data, financial institutions can enhance customer retention, customize marketing campaigns, and personalize their products. Big data analytics can also assist banks in identifying and reducing risks, spotting fraudulent activity, and improving regulatory compliance.

Similar to this, big data analytics is essential to the petroleum industry's optimization of production and exploration activities. Oil and gas businesses can enhance hydrocarbon recovery, optimize well performance, and find viable drilling sites by studying production parameters, well logs, and seismic data. Furthermore, predictive maintenance is made possible by big data analytics, which aids businesses in identifying equipment faults and refining maintenance plans to reduce downtime and increase operational efficiency.

But more is needed to fully utilize the power of big data than simply sophisticated analytics tools and technology. To guarantee the dependability, correctness, and security of their data assets, organizations must also invest in talent development, data governance frameworks, and data quality management. In addition, they need to take privacy and ethics into account to keep stakeholders and customers honest.

In summary, digital transformation is reinventing how businesses function, innovate, and interact with their clientele. It is also changing entire industries. Organizations can position themselves for success in an increasingly digital world by grasping the subtleties of digital transformation in a variety of industries, utilizing the power of digital banking, navigating digital disruption in the petroleum industry, and using big data for competitive advantage.

Part I: DETERMINING THE TRANSFORMATION STAGE

Success in the digital transformation path depends on building a solid foundation. The first section focuses on the crucial actions that companies need to take in order to prepare for change. This entails evaluating corporate culture, developing a digital transformation strategy for the banking sector, and updating procedures in the petroleum industry for the digital age.

Evaluating Organizational Culture

An essential first step in creating the framework for a successful digital transformation project is evaluating the corporate culture. Often called the "personality" of an organization, organizational culture consists of the common conventions, values, and behaviors that influence how people work and interact within it. For digital transformation initiatives to be driven and sustained, a culture that values creativity, cooperation, and adaptation is necessary.

Organizations must examine closely at several facets that impact attitudes and behaviors toward change in order to evaluate organizational culture. A key component is leadership style. The perceptions and actions of employees are greatly influenced by the acts and behaviors of leaders, who also set the tone for the culture of the firm. In addition to exhibiting a readiness to accept change and innovation themselves, leaders need to live up to the principles of experimentation, openness, and agility.

Organizational communication channels are also very important in forming culture. Clear and open lines of communication make it easier for ideas, information, and criticism to circulate, which promotes cooperation and trust. Leaders need to make sure that there is two-way communication and actively solicit opinions and participation from staff members across the board.

Furthermore, decision-making procedures might reveal information about the culture of a business. Workers in hierarchical companies with centralized decision-making may feel underpowered and hesitant to experiment or take chances. On the other hand, companies that delegate authority to staff members and allow them to make decisions on their own are more likely to promote an autonomous, creative, and flexible culture.

Consideration of employee attitudes toward change is another crucial element of company culture. It is normal for employees to be resistant to change, particularly when they believe that digital transformation projects may jeopardize their jobs or livelihoods. It is imperative for leaders to proactively address the concerns and fears of their employees by offering them support, comfort, and opportunity to become involved and participate in the change process.

Putting money into the training and development of staff members is crucial to creating a culture that welcomes digital transformation. Workers need to be prepared with the abilities, know-how, and competences required to adjust to new working practices and technological advancements. Employees may embrace change and help transformation projects succeed by developing their digital literacy and confidence with the support of training programs, workshops, and tools.

Organizations can cultivate an environment that is conducive to the success of digital transformation programs by evaluating and fostering a culture that prioritizes innovation, collaboration, and ongoing learning. Leaders need to set a good example by encouraging an atmosphere that values flexibility over rigidity, encourages experimentation, and views setbacks as teaching moments. Organizations can drive innovation, development, and competitive advantage in an increasingly digital environment by navigating the complexity of digital transformation with confidence and resilience when they have the proper culture in place.

Developing a Vision for Banking's Digital Revolution

Creating a vision for digital transformation in banking involves more than just implementing new technology or digital solutions; it involves radically rethinking how banks function, engage with their clientele, and generate value in an increasingly digital world. on addition to outlining a clear plan for utilizing digital technologies to spur innovation, expansion, and distinction, this vision needs to be grounded on a thorough grasp of consumer wants, market trends, and competitive dynamics.

The realization that digital transformation is now a need for survival and growth in today's quickly changing environment is at the core of developing a vision for digital transformation in banking. Technology is changing at a rapid pace, and fintech firms are becoming more and more competitive. These factors are transforming the banking sector, putting established business models to the test, and pressuring banks to change or risk going out of business.

Banks must first perform in-depth market research and analysis to obtain insights into client preferences, behaviors, and pain areas before crafting a strategy for digital transformation. In order to find chances for distinction and value creation, this entails obtaining client input, examining market trends, and comparing against industry best practices.

The organization's strategic goals and objectives should be in line with the ambitious but achievable vision for digital transformation. It ought to lay out a precise plan for utilizing digital technology to improve client experiences, expedite processes, and spur company expansion. This could involve projects like creating cutting-edge digital goods and services, enhancing omni-channel consumer interactions, and putting data-driven decision-making procedures in place.

Effective communication of the vision to all relevant parties, such as staff members, clients, investors, and regulators, is also vital. By presenting a convincing story that emphasizes the advantages of digital transformation and the value it offers to all stakeholders, leaders may inspire trust and dedication. In order to guarantee alignment and buy-in throughout the business, this calls for open communication, active participation, and continual discussion.

In order to achieve their strategic goals in the digital age, banks may mobilize support, align resources, and create momentum by developing a compelling and well-defined vision for digital transformation. While banks traverse the challenges of digital transformation and plot a course toward a more inventive, flexible, and customer-focused future, this vision acts as a beacon of light, giving them direction and purpose. In the end, the vision is what will motivate and enable banks to welcome change, grasp opportunities, and prosper in a world that is becoming more and more digital.

Modernizing Petroleum Sector Procedures for the Digital Age

The petroleum sector is undergoing a significant transition in the digital age, while historically being defined by its reliance on manual procedures and physical infrastructure. Every stage of the petroleum value chain is undergoing a transformation because to the rapid improvements in technology, including automation, the Internet of Things, and data analytics. This includes exploration, production, refining, and distribution.

Conducting a thorough evaluation of current systems, capabilities, and procedures is the first step towards modernizing petroleum sector operations for the digital age. Companies need to find ways to use digital technologies to improve productivity, make better decisions, and open up new value streams across the whole value chain.

For instance, IoT-enabled predictive maintenance can assist oil and gas firms in anticipating equipment problems and implementing preventative measures to minimize downtime and maximize asset performance. Similar to this, modern data analytics can offer insightful information on market trends, production performance, and reservoir features, helping businesses to maximize their production plans and make better judgments.

Furthermore, the petroleum business has a chance to embrace sustainability and lessen its environmental impact thanks to digital revolution. Oil and gas companies can reduce their environmental effect without sacrificing revenue or operational efficiency by utilizing renewable energy sources, putting energy-efficient technologies into place, and switching to cleaner production methods.

The path towards digital transformation is not without difficulties, though. A culture resistant to change, intricate legal frameworks, and legacy infrastructure can all obstruct the adoption of digital technology and transformational efforts. Furthermore, strong cybersecurity measures are necessary to protect against such breaches since cybersecurity attacks pose a serious risk to digital infrastructure and data integrity.

In conclusion, firms must evaluate their organizational culture, develop a clear vision, and modify industry standards for the digital age in order to prepare the ground for digital transformation. Organizations may set themselves up for success in a world going digital by embracing change, encouraging innovation, and utilizing digital technologies.

Part II: TECHNOLOGY FOUNDATIONS

Technology is the cornerstone on which creative ideas and operational efficiencies are constructed in the field of digital transformation. In Part II, "Technology

Foundations," the key technological elements that support effective transformation initiatives are examined. This part examines the use of digital platforms in banking operations, the petroleum industry's integration of IoT and automation, and the revolutionary potential of big data analytics in fostering creativity and insights.

Utilizing Digital Platforms for Banking Activities

The banking industry is faced with previously unheard-of opportunities and problems in the fast-paced world of today because to digital change. Banks now need to use digital platforms not just as a competitive advantage but also as a means of meeting client expectations, remaining relevant, and promoting operational excellence. These platforms cover a broad spectrum of technology and solutions that enable smooth interactions between banks, clients, staff, and partners, completely changing the way that banking activities are carried out.

The unwavering pursuit of providing clients with individualized and convenient services while streamlining internal procedures and workflows is the fundamental component of utilizing digital platforms in banking operations. With the ability to conduct a wide range of transactions from the convenience of their homes or while on the road, mobile banking apps and online banking portals have evolved into essential tools for consumers. With only a few taps on their smartphones or clicks on their laptops, clients can check account balances, transfer funds, pay bills, and apply for loans, among other chores. Digital channels not only improve the entire banking experience for clients by offering them more flexibility and convenience, but they also assist banks in cutting down on the operating costs of maintaining manual processes and traditional brick-and-mortar branches.

Digital platforms also help banks encourage better staff collaboration and communication, dismantling organizational silos and facilitating smooth departmental and branch coordination. The foundation of internal operations is provided by enterprise resource planning (ERP) systems, which combine several departments like supply chain management, finance, and human resources onto a unified platform. At every level of the company, this facilitates informed decision-making by giving real-time visibility into critical performance measures. In a similar vein, banks may centralize client data, monitor interactions, and customize services with the use of customer relationship management (CRM) platforms, which strengthens bonds with customers and increases loyalty.

Digital platforms not only enhance internal processes and customer experiences, but they also encourage innovation and agility in banks. Application programming interfaces (APIs) and open banking platforms make it easier for banks to work with fintech startups and outside developers, giving them access to a wide range of creative services and solutions. Banks may establish themselves as industry leaders and create value for stakeholders and customers by utilizing digital platforms.

Digital platforms also help banks respond quickly to shifting client demands and market realities, which promotes an agile and adaptable culture. Banks that can swiftly roll out new features, goods, and services will be able to outperform the competition and take advantage of new opportunities in the digital space. This flexibility is especially important in the quickly changing market of today, when disruptive technologies are redefining old company models and customer expectations are always changing.

To sum up, banks must take use of digital platforms if they want to prosper in the digital world. Banks may improve customer experiences, expedite processes, encourage innovation, and create value for both stakeholders and customers by adopting these technologies. But effectively utilizing digital platforms calls for a planned approach, financial support for talent acquisition and technology infrastructure, as well as a dedication to ongoing innovation and development. In an increasingly digital environment, banks may position themselves for long-term success by putting the correct digital platforms in place.

IoT and Automation in the Petroleum Industry

The petroleum industry has undergone a paradigm shift as a result of the integration of automation technology and Internet of Things (IoT) devices, completely changing how energy resources are discovered, extracted, and delivered. Along with automation technologies, the Internet of Things (IoT) is a network of networked devices embedded with sensors and communication solutions that is accelerating major improvements in environmental sustainability, safety, and operational efficiency throughout the petroleum value chain.

Investigation and Manufacturing:

IoT sensors placed in drilling rigs, pipelines, and offshore platforms act as the eyes and ears of the exploration and production industry, gathering data in real-time on vital factors like temperature, pressure, and flow rates. Due to the priceless insights this data offers on reservoir properties and production performance, businesses are better equipped to maximize resource recovery, minimize downtime, and optimize drilling operations. Businesses may use IoT to make data-driven decisions, reduce risks, and improve operational effectiveness, all of which help them become more profitable and competitive in a difficult market.

Automation technologies lower costs and streamline processes, which is a complement to IoT activities. By automating repetitive and rule-based processes like data input and regulatory compliance, robotic process automation (RPA) frees up human resources to concentrate on more strategic endeavors. In a similar vein, autonomous vehicles—such as drones and unmanned aerial vehicles—are used to remotely check and monitor vital infrastructure, like storage tanks, refineries, and pipelines. By lowering the need for human intervention in dangerous situations and lowering the possibility of mishaps and incidents, these technologies improve safety.

Regulatory compliance, environmental sustainability, and safety:

In the petroleum industry, IoT and automation technologies are essential for improving safety, environmental sustainability, and regulatory compliance in addition to operating efficiency. IoT sensors enable proactive intervention and mitigation actions by detecting and alerting operators to possible safety issues, such as gas leaks, equipment failures, and environmental incidents. In the event of an emergency, automation technologies, such as remote-controlled valves and shut-off systems, can be used to reduce environmental damage and prevent accidents, safeguarding both people and the environment.

IoT data analytics also make predictive maintenance solutions possible, which help businesses decrease downtime, maximize asset performance, and detect equipment faults before they happen. Businesses can minimize operational disruptions, increase asset longevity, and boost overall reliability by proactively addressing maintenance needs.

Opportunities and Difficulties:

Although automation and IoT technologies have many advantages, the petroleum industry has difficulties in using them. Among the main obstacles that businesses must overcome are needs for worker reskilling, interoperability, and data security and privacy concerns. A strategic strategy, as well as investments in personnel development, organizational change management, and technology infrastructure, are needed to overcome these obstacles.

In summary, the petroleum industry is changing as a result of the integration of IoT and automation technologies, which is promoting environmental sustainability, operational efficiency, and safety. Businesses can improve safety procedures, assure regulatory compliance, and streamline the exploration and production processes by utilizing these technology. To fully utilize IoT and automation, though, demands a determined effort to overcome obstacles and seize possibilities, which will ultimately propel value creation and long-term, steady growth in the petroleum sector.

Big Data Analytics

In today's data-driven economy, big data analytics has become a revolutionary force, enabling organizations in a wide range of industries to derive meaningful insights from large and diverse datasets. With the help of this effective tool, businesses may foster innovation, make well-informed decisions, and achieve a competitive advantage in a dynamic and more complex business environment. Let's examine in more detail how operations in the banking and petroleum industries are being transformed by big data analytics.

Within the Banking Sector:

Big data analytics is completely changing how banks see and interact with their clientele. Financial institutions can obtain more profound understanding of consumer behavior, preferences, and requirements by examining large amounts of transactional data, social media interactions, and demographic data. In the end, this helps banks to build deeper relationships and increase client loyalty by allowing them to personalize offers, optimize marketing campaigns, and enhance customer experiences.

Furthermore, big data analytics is essential to the banking sector's efforts to reduce risk and detect fraud. Banks should take proactive steps to safeguard consumer assets and uphold confidence in the financial system by using advanced analytics techniques like machine learning and predictive modeling to spot anomalies and trends suggestive of fraudulent activity.

Big data analytics also stimulates product creation and innovation in the banking industry. Banks are able to recognize new market opportunities and create cutting-edge products and services that cater to changing consumer preferences and demands by examining market trends, rival performance, and customer feedback. Predictive analytics, for instance, may evaluate creditworthiness and customize loan offers, allowing banks to increase credit availability while lowering risks.

Within the Petroleum Industry:

Exploration, production, and operational efficiency are all improving as a result of big data analytics' revolutionary impact on the petroleum industry. Businesses can find viable exploration locations, enhance drilling tactics, and enhance reservoir management procedures by evaluating data from seismic surveys, drilling operations, and production facilities. As a result, businesses are able to increase profitability, reduce expenses, and maximize resource recovery.

Additionally, big data analytics helps petroleum businesses anticipate equipment breakdowns, manage maintenance schedules, and enhance asset performance. Businesses may detect possible problems before they arise, enabling proactive maintenance and reducing downtime and production losses, by evaluating data from IoT sensors, maintenance logs, and operational factors.

Additionally, big data analytics is essential to improving environmental sustainability and safety in the petroleum industry. Businesses can identify patterns and trends that point to potential safety risks or environmental issues by evaluating data from sensors, monitoring systems, and environmental monitoring stations. In the end, this ensures worker safety and environmental protection by empowering businesses to take proactive steps to avoid mishaps, reduce risks, and lessen their negative effects on the environment.

In the banking and petroleum industries, big data analytics is revolutionizing operations by enhancing customer interaction, risk mitigation, operational effectiveness, and environmental sustainability. In a world where data is becoming more and more important, companies can remain ahead of the competition, spur innovation, and gain vital insights by utilizing big data analytics.

To sum up, big data analytics is a potent instrument that stimulates creativity and new ideas in the banking and petroleum industries. Organizations may improve operations, spur corporate growth, and have a deeper understanding of customer behavior by utilizing sophisticated analytics techniques and technology. But in order to fully utilize big data analytics, one must adopt a strategic approach, make investments in human development and technical infrastructure, and be dedicated to continual improvement and data-driven decision-making. Organizations can seize new chances for innovation, expansion, and competitive advantage in an increasingly digital world by utilizing big data analytics.

Part III: IMPROVING THE USER INTERFACE

User Experience (UX) has become a significant distinction for enterprises across industries in today's hyperconnected world. In Part III, "Enhancing User Experience," the key tactics and approaches for providing outstanding user experiences in the contexts of online banking and petroleum operations are examined. The fundamentals of design thinking for digital banking goods and services, user experience optimization in petroleum operations, and customized customer interaction methods are all covered in this section.

Design Thinking for Products and Services in Digital Banking

In many different industries, design thinking has become a key technique for encouraging creativity and creating solutions that are focused on the needs of the consumer. Design thinking is a methodical approach to comprehending, generating ideas, and executing novel products and services that effectively connect with users in the digital banking industry, where customer experience is of utmost importance. Let's examine more closely how excellent digital banking experiences are made by implementing design thinking ideas.

- Empathy: The capacity to comprehend and feel empathy with the requirements, actions, and motives of banking clients is the fundamental component of design thinking. Firstly, banks carry out comprehensive user research, journey mapping, and persona building exercises to acquire a comprehensive understanding of the varied requirements and challenges faced by their clientele. Through customer immersion, banks can gain important insights that form the basis for creating user-friendly, customer-focused products.

Banks may pinpoint important areas for improvement and pain spots in the customer journey—like laborious account opening procedures, perplexing digital banking app navigation, or a dearth of personalized services—by conducting empathy-driven research. With these data at hand, banks may better understand the requirements and goals of their clients, setting the stage for creating solutions that genuinely improve their quality of life.

- Ideation: Following the collection of insights, cross-functional teams convene to generate innovative ideas to tackle recognized problems and prospects. This cooperative strategy promotes unconventional thinking and an innovative culture within the company. Teams come up with a wide range of ideas and concepts through design workshops, sketching exercises, and brainstorming sessions that have the potential to revolutionize the digital banking experience.

During brainstorming meetings, a variety of options may be explored, such as reworking the user interface of mobile banking applications or adding new features targeted at particular clientele. The aim is to come up with creative solutions that satisfy client demands and complement the bank's strategic goals. Through the utilization of cross-functional teams' combined expertise and creativity, banks can discover new ways to solve client problems and improve the entire banking experience.

- Prototyping and Iteration: To bring concepts to life and get input from actual consumers, banks prototype their ideas using real-world tools like wireframes, mockups, or interactive prototypes. Banks can test hypotheses, validate concepts, and pinpoint areas for improvement early in the development process by using rapid prototyping. Banks may ensure that their prototypes fulfill customer expectations and needs by iteratively refining them based on feedback from users through user interviews and usability testing.

A fundamental component of design thinking is iterative development, which emphasizes learning via feedback loops and ongoing improvement. Banks can prioritize improvements and enhancements based on user feedback and market demand by using agile approaches like Scrum and Kanban. This helps to ensure that products and services adapt to changing customer needs and preferences. Banks may provide value to consumers rapidly and iteratively by adopting an experimentation and adaption approach, which promotes continual development in the digital banking experience.

- Implementation: Banks concentrate on making their concepts a reality and providing clients with value in a timely, iterative manner throughout this phase. Banks can accelerate time-to-market and increase flexibility in responding to changing requirements by using agile development approaches to break down complicated projects into smaller, more manageable pieces. Through the adoption of an agile mentality and a culture that values experimentation and learning, banks can provide their clients with digital banking products and services that are easy to use, captivating, and enjoyable.

In general, design thinking gives banks the ability to develop digital banking experiences that are genuinely focused on the needs of their customers, which helps them stand out from the competition in a crowded market. In the digital age, banks may create solutions that meet the changing requirements and preferences of their clients by embracing empathy, creativity, and iteration. This will strengthen client connections and propel corporate growth.

Enhancing User Interface for Petroleum Operations

In a business where people work in dangerous and complicated situations, protecting the safety of employees and equipment, optimizing resource usage, and assuring operational efficiency all depend on petroleum operations. Every facet of petroleum operations, including workflow procedures, monitoring systems, and equipment interfaces, from drilling rigs to refineries, is critical to achieving operational excellence. Let's examine the main tactics in more detail so that we may maximize user experience in petroleum operations.

User-friendly and intuitive interfaces:

Making equipment and control systems interfaces clear and easy to use is a fundamental part of maximizing user experience in petroleum operations. Human-machine interfaces, or HMIs, are the main tools used by operators to efficiently communicate with and operate complicated operations. Through the integration of ergonomics and usability principles into HMI design, businesses can decrease operator errors, improve operator performance, and lower cognitive burden.

Clear and simple layouts, simple navigation, and easily comprehensible symbols and icons are characteristics of intuitive HMIs. Because the end user is the primary focus of these interfaces, operators can readily obtain and interpret crucial information, enabling them to complete jobs quickly and effectively. Customization choices also let users adapt the interface to their own requirements and tastes, which improves usability and efficiency even more.

Real-time monitoring systems with IoT sensors:

Enhancing the user experience in petroleum operations can also be achieved through the integration of real-time monitoring systems and Internet of Things sensors. Real-time data on temperature, pressure, and flow rates is gathered via IoT sensors placed throughout the operational environment. After that, this data is sent to centralized monitoring systems, where it is handled, examined, and displayed using user-friendly dashboards and data analytics tools.

IoT sensors and monitoring systems enable operators to make educated decisions and take proactive steps to reduce risks and prevent downtime by giving them actionable information and alerts. For instance, sensors can identify abnormalities or departures from standard operating procedures and notify managers of any equipment malfunctions or safety risks, enabling prompt intervention and remedial measures.

Optimization of Workflow Process:

Another crucial component of improving user experience in petroleum operations is workflow process optimization. Businesses can increase productivity, lower the risk of human error, and improve operational efficiency by simplifying procedures, eliminating complexity, and automating repetitive jobs.

Businesses may automate time-consuming and repetitive operations with automation technologies like robotic process automation (RPA) and workflow optimization tools, freeing up human resources to concentrate on more strategic duties. RPA, for instance, can automate operations related to regulatory compliance, data input, and report preparation, lowering human error and increasing accuracy and efficiency.

In order to guarantee that operators have access to the appropriate information at the appropriate moment, workflow optimization also entails streamlining information flow and communication channels. Businesses may speed up decision-making and problem-solving by facilitating smooth communication and information exchange between operators, supervisors, and other stakeholders through the use of integrated communication systems and collaboration platforms.

All things considered, improving the user experience in petroleum operations necessitates a comprehensive strategy that includes process optimization, technology, and design. Companies may empower operators to do their duties efficiently, avoid downtime, and maximize resource utilization by placing a high priority on usability, efficiency, and safety. In the petroleum industry, businesses may stay competitive by utilizing IoT sensors, real-time monitoring systems, intuitive interfaces, and workflow optimization tools to achieve operational excellence.

Personalization Strategies for Customer Engagement

In today's competitive world, personalization has emerged as a critical approach for businesses in all sectors to effectively engage customers. Businesses may develop experiences that connect with consumers personally by customizing communications, services, and goods to fit their unique preferences and habits. This builds stronger bonds with clients and increases customer loyalty. Let's examine in more detail how customization techniques are used to improve client engagement and propel corporate success in the petroleum and digital banking industries.

Customization in Online Banking:

Personalization methods play a crucial role in providing clients with relevant and customized products in the digital banking domain, taking into account their financial needs, aspirations, and preferences. Banks are able to efficiently segment their client base and spot chances for personalization by using data analytics and machine learning algorithms to examine consumer transaction histories, demographics, and behavioral patterns.

Offering tailored product recommendations and promotions based on unique customer profiles and interests is one popular personalization tactic in digital banking. Banks are able to find chances for cross-selling and upselling as well as customize product suggestions to fit the needs and objectives of individual customers by examining transactional data and customer interactions. A bank might, for instance, provide a customer with a customized suggestion for a credit card or loan product based on their spending patterns and financial objectives.

Furthermore, personalization includes customized communication and engagement tactics in addition to product recommendations. Banks may provide personalized messages and offers that connect with each individual consumer by segmenting their clientele according to their interests, communication styles, and life events. This encourages interaction and loyalty. For example, on a customer's birthday or anniversary, a bank can give exclusive discounts or awards through tailored emails or push notifications as a way to show their thanks.

Customization in the Oil and Gas Industry:

Though in a slightly different setting, personalization techniques are being used more and more in the petroleum industry to improve consumer engagement and loyalty. To provide individualized services and support, companies in the petroleum industry use data analytics and Internet of Things (IoT) technologies to obtain insights into consumer preferences, consumption trends, and equipment performance.

Businesses, for instance, can provide equipment suggestions and customized maintenance schedules based on usage data from the past and predictive analytics. Businesses can identify maintenance needs and proactively plan service appointments, limiting downtime and maximizing equipment uptime for customers, by evaluating equipment performance parameters and maintenance histories.

Additionally, businesses can tailor communications and interactions with customers according on their preferences and usage habits. To keep consumers informed and involved, a petroleum firm, for example, can send them individualized alerts or notifications about impending maintenance jobs or service appointments.

In general, customization tactics help businesses in the banking and petroleum industries give their clients more relevant and meaningful experiences, which increases customer engagement, loyalty, and eventually, business success. Businesses may fully realize the benefits of personalization and stand out in a crowded market by utilizing data analytics, machine learning, and consumer insights. Whether it is applied to digital banking or oilfield operations, personalization is still a potent tool for building longer-lasting relationships with customers and promoting growth.

Part IV: FOSTERING AN DIGITAL CULTURE

To prosper and stay competitive in the ever changing digital market, enterprises must foster a digital culture. Important tactics for developing a digital culture in banking and petroleum companies are covered in Part IV. This covers leadership techniques for encouraging innovation, pushing digital adoption, and retraining workers in digital competency.

Effective Leadership Techniques to Promote Digital Adoption

Organizations must use leadership techniques to drive digital adoption in order to successfully navigate the challenges of digital transformation. Here, we go into further detail about each essential component of successful leadership in encouraging digital adoption:

1. Visionary Leadership: By presenting a compelling vision for the organization's digital future, visionary leaders play a crucial role in promoting digital adoption. They inspire staff members to welcome change and coordinate their efforts with the strategic objectives of the company by outlining the advantages and prospects of the digital transformation. Visionary leaders set an example for others to follow by committing themselves to digital initiatives in both their choices and actions. Visionary leaders arouse excitement and encourage staff members to actively engage in the transformation process by providing a clear picture of the future state made possible by digital technology.

2. Change Management: During the digital transformation process, change management is essential for overcoming resistance and guaranteeing seamless transitions. Proficient leaders recognize the

significance of attending to issues, maintaining open lines of communication, and offering assistance to staff members during the transition period. By stressing the dangers of sticking with the status quo and the benefits of welcoming change, they instill a sense of urgency for the adoption of digital technology. Additionally, leaders encourage a sense of ownership and commitment to digital initiatives by involving stakeholders at all organizational levels in the decision-making process. Leaders create the conditions for successful digital adoption and deployment by proactively addressing resistance.

3. Empowerment and Collaboration: Promoting a culture of continuous improvement and accelerating digital adoption require giving staff members the freedom to innovate and work together. Supervisors establish a work atmosphere where staff members are encouraged to try out novel concepts and tools, take measured chances, and grow from mistakes. By dismantling organizational silos and encouraging open lines of communication between teams and departments, they enhance cross-functional collaboration. Leaders can unleash the combined creativity and expertise of their workforce, propelling innovation and quickening the adoption of digital technologies, by promoting knowledge sharing, cooperation, and teamwork.

4. Investment in Talent: Developing internal digital capabilities and guaranteeing the accomplishment of digital projects depend on investing in talent. Hiring and developing personnel with the digital skills and capabilities required to achieve transformation is a top priority for leaders. They offer chances for current staff members to retrain and upskill in order to close the skills gap in digital technology and get them ready for the demands of the modern workplace. Additionally, leaders foster an environment that values lifelong learning and professional advancement, encouraging staff members to pick up new skills and keep abreast of market developments and developing technologies. Leaders who make talent development investments enable their staff to embrace digital transformation and foster creativity throughout the company.

In conclusion, strong leadership is essential to promoting digital transformation and adoption in businesses. Through the adoption of visionary leadership, proficient change management, talent investment, and empowerment, leaders can cultivate an innovative culture and spearhead triumphant digital initiatives, thereby situating their businesses for prosperity in the digital age.

Encouraging Innovation in Petroleum and Banking Sectors

Organizations working in fast-paced industries like banking and petroleum, where staying ahead of the curve is critical for long-term success, must foster innovation. Below is a more thorough examination of the tactics used to promote innovation in both industries:

1. Promoting Innovation and Creativity: Innovation flourishes in settings that promote creativity and embrace experimentation. Companies in the banking and petroleum industries should foster a culture that encourages staff members to experiment, take measured risks, and learn from mistakes. By encouraging a healthy environment for innovation and pushing staff members to question the status quo and think creatively, leaders play a critical role in establishing the tone. Offering employees the chance to express their creativity through hackathons, innovation challenges, or brainstorming sessions promotes an innovative culture.

2. Cross-Functional Collaboration: In complex organizations, innovation is driven by cross-disciplinary and departmental collaboration. Innovative digital banking solutions can be developed in the banking industry through cooperation between the marketing, technology, and product development teams. Similar to this, in the petroleum sector, cooperation between operations, data science, and engineering teams can spur innovation in the processes

of production, exploration, and refining. Organizations can address difficult challenges and spur innovation by leveraging multiple views and skill sets through the dismantling of organizational silos and the promotion of cross-functional collaboration.

3. Investing in Research and Development: To spur innovation and maintain a competitive edge, research and development (R&D) spending is essential. Organizations in the banking and petroleum sectors invest money in investigating novel technology, business strategies, and market prospects. Organizations invest in innovation labs, incubators, and accelerators to create game-changing ideas, whether they are creating new fintech solutions for the banking industry or investigating cutting edge drilling techniques for the petroleum sector. Organizations support R&D efforts that result in inventions that change the game by encouraging a culture of experimentation and providing the required resources and support.

4. Collaborations and Environments: Encouraging innovation through strategic collaboration with external partners such as startups, academic institutions, and industry peers is a viable way. Organizations in the banking and petroleum sectors use strategic alliances and partnerships to enter new markets, obtain insights into developing trends, and obtain access to outside expertise. Organizations work

with research institutions to investigate renewable energy technologies or fintech startups to build creative banking solutions. By cooperating with external ecosystems, they can drive co-innovation and expedite their innovation agenda.

Banking and petroleum companies may leverage the full potential of their staff, promote continuous improvement, and maintain a competitive edge in a constantly changing environment by adopting these innovation-fostering tactics. Organizations that embrace innovation are better positioned for long-term success in the digital economy as it becomes a critical driver of growth, differentiation, and sustainability.

Retraining Employees in Digital Competence

Retraining the workforce for digital competency is crucial as businesses embrace digital transformation, ensuring that workers have the knowledge, abilities, and skills needed to thrive in the digital era. The following are crucial tactics for reskilling the labor force:

1. Finding Skill Gaps: To determine what areas require more training and development for personnel, organizations carry out skills assessments and gap analyses. Organizations can customize reskilling initiatives to meet particular requirements and goals by

having a thorough awareness of the present skill levels of their workforce.

2. Providing Training and Development Programs: Businesses provide training and development courses that concentrate on digital competencies and abilities, including cybersecurity, data analytics, artificial intelligence, and digital marketing. To improve staff competencies, these programs could include webinars, workshops, certificates, and online courses.

3. Promoting Continuous Learning: Companies support a professional development and learning culture that empowers staff members to take charge of their own education. Leaders give their staff members the chance to learn new skills, experiment with cutting-edge technologies, and keep current with best practices and trends in the field.

4. Encouraging Cross-Functional Mobility: To give employees exposure to a variety of jobs and areas of expertise, organizations encourage cross-functional mobility as well as internal career development possibilities. Organizations enable employees to expand their skill sets and perspectives by offering mentorship programs, job rotations, and secondments.

5. Acknowledging and Rewarding Learning: Companies honor and reward staff members who show a dedication to their professional growth. Employees are

encouraged to participate in their professional development by their businesses through career progression opportunities, career celebrations, and feedback.

Organizations may enable their employees to adjust to changing job responsibilities and technology improvements and stay competitive and future-ready in the digital economy by investing in reskilling and upskilling efforts.

In conclusion, companies must develop a digital culture if they want to prosper in the quickly changing digital environment of today. In Part IV, important tactics for creating a digital culture in banking and petroleum companies are examined. These tactics include leadership techniques for promoting innovation, encouraging digital adoption, and retraining employees to become digitally competent. Organizations may position themselves for success in the digital age by adopting visionary leadership, encouraging innovation, and investing in staff development. This will help them to create a culture of continual learning, experimentation, and adaptation.

Part V: IMPLEMENTATION AND EXECUTION

Organizations must successfully implement and carry out digital transformation projects in order to fulfill their strategic goals and realize their vision. In Part V, important implementation and execution topics are covered, such as managing digital transformation projects at scale, overcoming change opposition in the petroleum industry, and using agile approaches for digital projects in banking.

Agile Project Management Techniques for Digital Banking

Agile approaches have revolutionized the way banks approach software development and digital transformation initiatives, becoming the cornerstone of digital projects in the banking sector. These approaches—which include Scrum and Kanban—provide a framework that is adaptable and agile, allowing banks to efficiently react to shifting client preferences, market demands, and technology improvements. Let's examine the main ideas and procedures of agile approaches for digital banking projects in more detail:

1. Iterative Development: Agile approaches support the division of projects into smaller, more manageable units called sprints or iterations. Usually lasting a few weeks, each iteration produces a possibly shippable product increment. Banks can release functionality incrementally with this iterative strategy, collecting input from customers and stakeholders at the conclusion of each sprint. Banks may make sure the final product meets consumer expectations and corporate goals by incorporating input into successive revisions.

2. Cross-Functional Teams: Agile teams in the banking industry are made up of individuals with a variety of skill sets, such as business analysts, testers, developers,

and designers. From project conception to completion, these cross-functional teams work closely together to foster shared ownership, knowledge exchange, and group accountability for project outcomes. Agile teams facilitate innovation, expedite decision-making, and expedite the time-to-market for digital products and services by assembling individuals with disparate viewpoints and specialties.

3. Customer-Centricity: Agile approaches in banking place a strong emphasis on customer input and cooperation. Agile teams place a high priority on learning about the wants, needs, and pain points of their customers in order to make sure that digital goods and services live up to their expectations. Banks can obtain insights and validate assumptions frequently by involving customers in the development process through techniques like usability testing, feedback loops, and user research. Banks may improve features and capabilities to create value that resonates with end users and increases customer satisfaction and loyalty by incorporating feedback from customers into the development cycle.

4. Continuous Improvement: Teams that use agile approaches are encouraged to adopt a culture of continuous improvement, where they evaluate their operations, pinpoint areas for improvement, and modify their procedures as necessary. At the conclusion of every iteration, teams have a regular retrospective

where they discuss what went well, what didn't, and how they can get better. Agile teams in banking may continuously improve their digital goods and services and remain responsive to changing market conditions and client expectations by accepting feedback and learning from both triumphs and failures.

Agile approaches have, in general, changed the way banks handle digital initiatives, allowing them to provide excellent goods and services that satisfy changing client demands and increase shareholder value. Banks can successfully manage the challenges of digital transformation by adopting iterative development, cross-functional cooperation, customer-centricity, and continuous improvement. This will position them in an increasingly competitive landscape.

Overcoming Resistance to Change in the Petroleum Industry

Navigating the challenges of digital transformation in the petroleum business effectively requires overcoming opposition to change. In a sector where cultural norms, legacy systems, and deeply ingrained procedures are common, confronting resistance calls for proactive leadership, skillful communication, and stakeholder involvement. The following are some tactics for getting through the petroleum industry's opposition to change:

1. Explain the Reasoning: Overcoming opposition to change requires effective communication above all else. The benefits and opportunities that digital transformation projects provide to the company must be emphasized by leaders as they explain the reasoning behind them. Leaders may foster support and alignment among stakeholders by presenting a compelling future vision and aggressively addressing concerns. This will help people comprehend the necessity of change and its benefits for the firm.

2. Involve Stakeholders: To foster ownership and buy-in for digital transformation projects, early stakeholder involvement in the decision-making process is crucial. In order to understand their viewpoints, solve their issues, and collaboratively develop solutions that satisfy their needs, leaders should proactively solicit feedback from staff members, frontline workers, and other important stakeholders. Leaders may encourage a sense of ownership and commitment among stakeholders by integrating them in the change process. This will encourage participation and collaboration all the way through the transformation process.

3. Offer Resources and Support: Change can be intimidating, particularly for staff members used to conventional working practices. In order to assist staff members in navigating the shift and gaining the abilities and information required to thrive in the digital era, leaders must offer sufficient tools and

assistance. This could entail providing access to technical help, mentorship, coaching, and extensive training programs. Leaders show their dedication to their achievement and provide their staff the confidence to accept change by making investments in their professional development.

4. Celebrate Successes: Raising spirits and reiterating the benefits of change need acknowledging and applauding accomplishments made along the path to digital transformation. Whether it's bringing a new technology to market effectively, hitting important milestones, or providing value to customers, leaders should recognize and celebrate success. Celebrating accomplishments allows CEOs to instill self-assurance and drive, which in turn promotes an innovative and continuous improvement culture within the company.

In conclusion, overcoming the petroleum industry's reluctance to change necessitates a multidimensional strategy that places an emphasis on effective communication, stakeholder engagement, support, and success celebration. Through proactive problem-solving, stakeholder engagement, resource and support provision, and accomplishment recognition, executives may effectively manage resistance and steer prosperous digital transformation efforts within the petroleum sector.

Overseeing Digital Transformation Initiatives at Large

Large-scale digital transformation project management calls for a well-organized strategy, strong governance, and efficient project management techniques. Organizations facing significant digital projects must deal with issues of collaboration, scale, and complexity. The following tactics can be used to oversee large-scale digital transformation projects:

- Define Clear Objectives: To direct digital transformation initiatives and coordinate activities throughout the company, clear objectives are crucial. Each project needs a defined set of objectives, benchmarks, and success criteria that are specified by the leader to make that the organization's strategic priorities and intended results are met. Leaders give teams a road map for success and help them concentrate on adding value by setting clear objectives.

- Adopt Agile Practices: Scrum and Kanban are two agile approaches that work well for large-scale digital transformation project management. Agile techniques help organizations to deliver value gradually, avoid risks, and adapt to changing requirements by breaking down projects into smaller, more manageable chunks and accelerating time-to-market. Agile approaches encourage cooperation, creativity, and continual improvement, which propels project success at scale. Examples of these approaches include iterative development, cross-functional teams, and customer-centricity.

- Establish Robust Governance: Ensuring alignment with company goals and priorities and managing digital transformation projects require strong governance frameworks. In order to effectively oversee digital transformation programs, leaders need to define roles, responsibilities, and decision-making procedures. Throughout the course of a project, governance processes help businesses manage risks, address problems, and make well-informed decisions by offering supervision, accountability, and transparency.

- Encourage Collaboration and Communication: In large, geographically distributed enterprises, specifically, collaboration and communication are essential for conducting digital transformation projects at scale. In order for teams to effectively collaborate and work toward shared objectives, leaders must promote a culture of open communication, teamwork, and information sharing. Regardless of physical location, real-time cooperation and coordination are made easier by utilizing collaboration solutions including project management software, communication platforms, and virtual collaboration tools.

To sum up, the successful implementation and execution of digital transformation initiatives necessitate a comprehensive strategy that takes into account the particular possibilities and challenges faced by every firm. Organizations can lead effective digital transformation efforts that generate innovation, deliver value, and position them for long-term success in the digital age by embracing agile approaches, overcoming opposition to change, and putting strong governance structures in place.

Part VI: BEYOND DIGITAL TRANSFORMATION

Organizations operating in the dynamic fields of banking and petroleum must not only successfully negotiate the intricacies of digital transformation, but also take into account wider ethical considerations, predict emerging trends, and learn from successful case studies. Section VI delves into these facets, illuminating the moral implications, forthcoming patterns, and insightful insights garnered from prosperous digital revolutions.

Ethical Aspects in Banking and Petroleum Operations

Organizations in the banking and petroleum industries base a lot of their decisions and activities on ethical issues. Ethical behavior is not only morally required in these fields, but it is also necessary to preserve sustainability, reputation, and confidence. Let's examine the ethical aspects of banking and petroleum operations in more detail and consider how businesses might successfully handle these challenging situations.

1. Banking:

Given the banking industry's significant influence on people, companies, and the overall economy, a wide range of ethical issues are taken into account in this sector. Among the most important moral factors in banking are:

- Responsible Lending Practices: It is the duty of banks to guarantee that their lending policies are just, open, and in line with borrowers' best interests. This entails carrying out in-depth evaluations of borrowers' creditworthiness, giving borrowers precise information about the terms and conditions of the loan, and providing borrowers with the necessary financial guidance and support to enable them to make wise decisions.

- Data Security and Privacy: As banking services become more digitally connected, data security and privacy are becoming more and more crucial ethical issues. Maintaining the highest standards of cybersecurity and data protection is imperative for banks in order to protect client data from misuse, illegal access, and breaches. To protect sensitive financial data, this entails putting in place strong encryption methods, multi-factor authentication, and strict access limits.

- Financial Inclusion: Another moral requirement for banks is to guarantee fair access to financial services. Economic marginalization and disadvantaged groups are disproportionately affected by financial exclusion, which exacerbates socioeconomic inequality. It is the duty of banks to advance financial inclusion by providing easily accessible, reasonably priced, and customized financial products and services that cater to a variety of clientele, such as small enterprises, low-income individuals, and rural areas.

2. Activities Related to Petroleum:

Social responsibility, ethical corporate practices, and environmental stewardship are the main ethical factors in the petroleum industry. Owing to the industry's substantial influence on the environment, nearby populations, and worldwide climate change, oil and gas firms are subject to increased scrutiny and accountability for their conduct. Among the most important moral factors in petroleum operations are:

- Environmental Stewardship: The extraction, production, and transportation of oil and gas have the potential to have a negative influence on the environment, including contamination of the air and water, destruction of habitats, and climate change. By minimizing greenhouse gas emissions, adopting best practices for resource extraction, and making investments in renewable energy alternatives, ethical oil and gas corporations prioritize environmental sustainability. In order to reduce and eliminate environmental harm, they also follow strict environmental norms and standards.

- Social Responsibility: Because oil and gas operations frequently affect native American territories, nearby populations, and culturally significant locations, they raise moral questions about community involvement, land rights, and human rights. Ethical businesses respect the rights, customs, and cultural heritage of local communities and indigenous peoples by having meaningful conversations and consultations with them. Additionally, they provide top priority to social development programs that improve the prosperity and well-being of host communities, such as infrastructure, healthcare, and education.

- Ethical company Practices: The petroleum sector depends on upholding ethical standards in company operations to preserve integrity and confidence. Integrity, honesty, and transparency are the cornerstones of ethical oil and gas companies' interactions with suppliers, consumers, governments, and regulators. They pledge to uphold fair competition, legal compliance, and best practices for corporate governance instead of participating in dishonest business practices, bribery, or unethical behavior.

Incorporating corporate culture, governance, and stakeholder engagement into banking and petroleum operations is just one aspect of the comprehensive and proactive strategy needed to address ethical concerns. Organizations that want to cultivate a culture of integrity, accountability, and social responsibility must include ethical concepts into their basic beliefs, policies, and decision-making procedures. Banks and petroleum businesses can produce sustainable value for society and future generations by adhering to ethical standards and enhancing their reputation.

Prospects for the Future of Petroleum Technologies and Digital Banking

Future developments in technology, shifting consumer expectations, and shifting market dynamics will all have an impact on banking and petroleum operations. In the upcoming years, a number of significant developments that will spur innovation, disruption, and change will reshape these industries.

Artificial intelligence (AI), machine learning, and blockchain technologies are predicted to become more widely used in digital banking, allowing banks to improve client experiences, streamline processes, and reduce risks. Artificial intelligence (AI)-driven chatbots and virtual assistants are transforming customer service by offering 24/7 individualized help and support. Banks may now make choices more quickly and accurately by utilizing machine learning algorithms for risk management, fraud detection, and credit scoring. Blockchain technology has the potential to completely transform the financial industry by enabling peer-to-peer transactions that are safe, transparent, and decentralized without the need for middlemen.

Furthermore, as banks embrace cooperation, interoperability, and ecosystem development, open banking and platformization are changing the face of the banking industry. Open banking programs encourage innovation and competition in the financial services sector by allowing consumers to safely share their financial information with outside suppliers. Platformization is the term used to describe the rise of banking platforms that give a large selection of goods and services from several suppliers, giving users more convenience, personalization, and choice.

Digital technologies like automation, IoT, and data analytics are driving innovation and efficiency in the petroleum industry along the whole value chain. Companies may save costs, increase operational efficiency, and optimize exploration and production activities with the use of data analytics tools. IoT sensors are used in refineries, pipelines, and drilling rigs to gather data on equipment performance in real-time. This data enables proactive intervention and predictive maintenance to reduce risks and prevent downtime. Automation technologies that improve safety and productivity in hazardous situations include robotics and drones, which are revolutionizing inspection, monitoring, and maintenance tasks.

In the petroleum industry, renewable energy sources and sustainability programs are also becoming increasingly popular as businesses adapt to regulatory challenges and growing environmental concerns. In an effort to diversify their energy portfolios and lower their carbon footprint, businesses are increasingly investing in energy transition programs, renewable energy projects, and carbon capture and storage technology.

In general, digital transformation, sustainability, and technological innovation will define the future of banking and petroleum operations. Enterprises that adopt these patterns and adjust to the evolving environment will be in a strong position to prosper in the future digital economy.

Case Studies: Insights from Effective Digital Revolutions

Case studies of effective digital transformations offer priceless insights into the tactics, difficulties, and results that businesses encounter when they go through big changes. Organizations starting their digital transformation journeys can learn practical lessons and best practices by looking at real-world examples from the banking and petroleum industries.

1. DBS Bank's Digital Transformation: One notable instance of a banking industry digital transformation that has been effective is DBS Bank in Singapore. Using technology, analytics, and design thinking to reinvent customer banking experiences was the bank's transformation journey's main goal. The following are some important tactics that helped DBS Bank succeed:
- Customer-Centric Innovation: DBS Bank developed cutting-edge products and services that addressed pain points and provided value by giving priority to the requirements and preferences of its customers.
- Agile processes: DBS Bank was able to efficiently adapt to shifting market demands, deliver value progressively, and iterate rapidly after implementing agile processes.

- Digital Platforms: To give consumers a smooth and convenient banking experience, DBS Bank has made investments in digital platforms such online portals and mobile banking apps.
- Leadership Commitment: Top executives' advocacy of an innovative and customer-centric culture was important in propelling DBS Bank's digital transformation.

2. ING Bank's Agile Transformation: To speed its digital transformation initiatives and promote a culture of cooperation and continuous improvement, ING Bank in the Netherlands set out to implement agile methodology. Important takeaways from the agile transformation of ING Bank comprise:

- Cross-Functional Teams: To promote cooperation and shared project ownership, ING Bank established cross-functional teams with members that possessed a variety of skill sets.
- Iterative Development: ING Bank was able to obtain input from stakeholders, produce value gradually, and quickly adjust to changing requirements thanks to agile approaches.
- Empowered Workers: By giving workers the freedom to decide for themselves, ING Bank encouraged a sense of accountability and ownership for the results of projects.
- Continuous Learning: Employee upskilling and the development of digital capabilities were given top

priority by ING Bank, which provided resources and training in this area.

3. Shell's Digitization Initiatives: As a front-runner in the energy sector, Shell set out to change its operations digitally by utilizing automation, artificial intelligence, and data analytics to improve decision-making throughout its whole worldwide network. Important takeaways from Shell's digitization efforts consist of:
- Data-Driven Decision-Making: Shell adopted a data-driven strategy for making decisions, utilizing sophisticated analytics to uncover areas for optimization and provide insights into operational performance.
- Collaborative Innovation: Shell promoted a collaborative innovation culture by working with startups and technology firms to create and execute digital solutions that solved business problems.
- Safety and Sustainability: As part of its digitalization initiatives, Shell gave priority to safety and sustainability, putting in place procedures and technologies to boost regulatory compliance, lower environmental impact, and increase operational safety.
- Leadership Commitment: Shell's digital transformation was greatly aided by the executive leadership, which provided the resources, support, and vision required for the project to succeed.

These case studies demonstrate the value of customer-centric innovation, agile methodology, teamwork, and visionary leadership in facilitating effective digital revolutions in the banking and petroleum industries. Organizations can get valuable insights and best practices to guide their own digital transformation programs, achieve sustainable development, and remain competitive in the digital era by analyzing these real-world examples.

Part VI, which concludes, examines the wider implications of digital transformation in banking and petroleum operations, emphasizing lessons from successful case studies, future trends, and ethical issues. Organizations may effectively negotiate the difficulties of digital transformation and promote sustainable growth and innovation in the digital age by addressing ethical considerations, forecasting future trends, and drawing insights from real-world experiences.

CONCLUSION

Embracing the Digital Future Across Industries

The digital revolution is still reshaping industries worldwide as the twenty-first century goes on, changing how businesses run, engage with their clients, and spur innovation. Organizations must accept change, adjust to new technology, and rethink business models in order to succeed in the digital age. This applies to everything from banking to petroleum operations. The digital future offers previously unheard-of opportunities and problems.

In conclusion, companies must embrace the digital future across all industries if they want to be resilient, competitive, and relevant in a world that is changing quickly. A number of important themes and imperatives are involved in the journey towards digital transformation, and each of these is vital in determining the direction that companies hoping to prosper in the digital age should take.

Digital transformation starts, first and foremost, with a mentality shift in which businesses realize they must welcome change, question the status quo, and give priority to innovation and agility. Setting the example from the top and motivating staff to accept change, try new things, and push the envelope of what is possible are all made possible by visionary leadership, which is crucial for accelerating the adoption and transformation of digital technology.

Furthermore, in their efforts to undergo digital transformation, firms must give top priority to customer-centricity, putting the wants, needs, and experiences of their consumers front and center in the decision-making process. Organizations may enhance customer happiness and loyalty by delivering smooth and intuitive experiences, personalizing offers, and gaining deeper insights into customer behavior through the utilization of digital platforms, artificial intelligence, and data analytics.

In the digital age, collaboration and partnerships are especially important as companies want to harness the combined knowledge, assets, and skills of external stakeholders including financial companies, tech suppliers, and other industry players. With the help of strategic alliances, businesses may enter new markets, work together to produce creative solutions, and expand their ecosystem, opening up new avenues for expansion and value generation.

Additionally, in order to create digital capabilities and guarantee that staff members have the competencies required to thrive in the digital era, companies must engage in talent development and reskilling programs as part of their digital transformation efforts. Organizations may empower people to adopt new technologies, adjust to shifting roles and responsibilities, and foster creativity and competitiveness by placing a high priority on continuous learning and development.

Digital transformation is propelling the banking sector toward personalized services, digital banking platforms, and agile techniques that let banks provide value to clients rapidly and often. Banks can become leaders in the digital revolution by adopting digital platforms to improve client experiences, drive innovation, and streamline operations.

Comparably, digital transformation is transforming the exploration, extraction, and distribution of energy resources in the petroleum industry. By combining automation, data analytics, and the Internet of Things, businesses are able to increase environmental sustainability, optimize operations, and improve safety. Petroleum firms may enhance their operational efficiency, optimize resource use, and reduce risks by adopting digital technologies. This will help them remain competitive and viable in the continuously changing energy sector.

In conclusion, companies looking to prosper in the digital era must embrace the digital future across all industries. It is not only a matter of choice. Organizations may successfully traverse the challenges of digital transformation and seize new opportunities for growth, differentiation, and value creation in an increasingly digital environment by placing a high priority on innovation, customer-centricity, collaboration, and talent development. In order for companies to stay ahead of the curve in the digital world, they must accept change, adapt to new realities, and constantly reinvent themselves. This is a continual and always changing journey towards digital transformation.

www.ingramcontent.com/pod-product-compliance
Lightning Source LLC
Chambersburg PA
CBHW070359230526
45471CB00006B/2647